The Square Footage of Awe

The Square Footage of Awe

Poems by

Katrin Talbot

© 2025 Katrin Talbot. All rights reserved.
This material may not be reproduced in any form, published,
reprinted, recorded, performed, broadcast,
rewritten or redistributed without
the explicit permission of Katrin Talbot.
All such actions are strictly prohibited by law.

Cover design by Shay Culligan
Cover image "Self Portrait with Cumulus" by Katrin Talbot,
Renée Gouaux, and Jay Lichtmann
Author photo by Ariana Karp

ISBN: 978-1-63980-785-7

Kelsay Books
502 South 1040 East, A-119
American Fork, Utah 84003
Kelsaybooks.com

Just last week, I gasped at a sculpture. Jaw dropped, the whole kit and caboodle; I laughed at how brilliant it was. In a Schubert symphony, I've played moments that define something I've only encountered there, a velvet depth, a dark reverence. And the peach just carried down the hill from the tree. An owl's dusk calling. First words. Pretty much anything in the sky, day or night. The sound of a blizzard howling.

Unmeasurable awe.

I dedicate these poems to my father, James Talbot, and to my late mother, Margot Fetz, who gave me a simply astonishing life in four countries. My remarkable sisters, Gretchen and Susan, stalwart compatriots in these journeys, also get a dedicated kiss. This collection honours those in my life who have taken or continue to take my breath away. Please keep up the good and hard work of living and loving.

Acknowledgments

Thank you to the following publications, in which versions of these poems previously appeared:

Art Lit Lab: "Vaccination with Anna"
The Green Shoe Sanctuary: "The Naming," "Aspirational Fashion"
impspired: "The Bathtub of Coriolanus," "Hemming Caesar's Trousers," "Today You Are a Museum Wing"
Moss Piglet: "Toasted," "Self-Portrait," "Unseasonably," "Along the Interstate," "Minus Six and I Make Tea"
noun'd vb (dancing girl press, 2014): "Raven"
Qantara House: Hope Anthology: "It was Edna who Told Me," "Oz"
The Ravensperch: "In Which I Carry Lightning on my Back," "The Square Footage of Awe," "Clean Death"
Silver Birch Press: "Clothespin Nightlife"
Movement: Our Bodies in Action (Sweetycat Press, 2022): "Trill"
Verse Virtual: "Along the Santa Fe Trail," "Breakdown," "In the High Desert Pool," "Eldorado Nights," "Red Onion Politic," "Bass at Rest"
Your Daily Poem: "Garden Experiment Number Seventy-Two," "My Daughter Laughed"

Contents

I. Prism

Ice Storm	17
In Which I Carry Lightning on My Back	18
Toasted	19
Listening to Reels with a One-Hundred-and-Three-Year-Old	20
It Was Edna Who Told Me To	22
The Bathtub of Coriolanus	23
Adaptation	24
Along the Santa Fe Trail	25
Accessory to Love	26
Free Verse	27
Prism	28
Breakdown	29
At Three a.m.	30
Name Change	31
The Square Footage of Awe	32
First Loss	33
Oz	34
The Assassin's Son	36
Eating the Angel's Book	37
For a Friend in Tasmania	39
Viola Lessons	40
Yesterday	41
After Reading That Cows Have BFF's	42
The Fade	43
Occasional Purpose	44
Moose Sighting	45
Watching	46
Parameters	47

II. Fourteen Acorns and a Vagary

Before the Prologue	51
The Art of Dazzle	52
Packing for Bucharest	53
Journey of Flour Butter Sugar	54
Blue	55
Turning the Late Winter Blues into Red and Yellow	56
The Falling	57
The Naming	58
Last night	59
Wild Girl	60
If You Go Down Under	61
Fourteen Acorns and a Vagary	62
Garden Experiment Number Seventy-Two	63
At the Aquarium	64
Hemming Caesar's Trousers	65
Today You Are a Museum Wing	66
Finding	67
Vaccination with Anna	68
Storm While Hiking	70
Self-Portrait	71
Behemoth	72
Lined	73
Alive	74

III. Plainsong

Translation	77
Rumours of Dementia	78
Caught	79
My Daughter Laughed	80
Clothespin Nightlife	81
A Brief Brief History of a Snowball	82
The Gathering	83
Plainsong	84
Raven	86
The Bone's Story	87
Burying the Cat	88
A Close Read	89
Two Pairs	90
In the High Desert Pool	91
Eldorado Nights	92
Out Here	93
Unseasonably	94
Clean Death	95
Flamed	96
I Remember	97
Diversion	98
Red Onion Politic	99
Bass at Rest	100
Trill	101
Along the Interstate,	102
In the Hills Above Santa Fe	103
Minus Six and I Make Tea	104
Aspirational Fashion	105
Tonight	106

Watch the stars, and see yourself running with them.

—Marcus Aurelius, *Meditations*

I. Prism

Ice Storm

It's hitting the window like
bits of glass, gossiping
Glass against glass,
surface rapture

Schools are closed
to minimize broken bones

And we are left to sit and
listen, a soundtrack that
arrives only a few times a year,
percussive and
emphasizing gratitude for
a warm shelter

All day, the ice builds
and builds a surface,
like an ecstasy,
certain to
melt away

In Which I Carry Lightning on My Back

Up the mountain,
where the rock
bares its secrets
and I breathe in the earth
without a filter,
where *stoic* is the only name
for the trees who take
what is given to them
every season,
I find the black,
the white,
I carry them
down the mountain,
the story of lightning
in the charred wood,
the wisdom of the
bleached bone
and, after the descent,
I take the wood,
whose centuries-old essence
changed in a flash,
and write on the bone
STRUCK

Toasted

The Romans *spread* the idea,
a means to preserve,
Monsieur Maillard's reaction between
the reducing sugars and amino acids,
and my geologist father,
out in the bush,
managed to always
burn it in the manner of
the morning pancakes
but who cares
when you are eating by
any campfire under
South Australian stars?

Listening to Reels with a One-Hundred-and-Three-Year-Old

Betty with that constant gentle smile
who shows up to
every opera showing,
every racy foreign film

Her tiny frame carries
the years' magnificent weight
with so little effort

This is her one-hundred-and third St. Patrick's Day
and the band has come again
to the Willows

The accordion player, a luminous leader;
the singer forgets her words,
which could be in Gaelic or
English, we can't really tell

Over-mic'd, the guitarist
will soon have back problems,
and the fiddler always seems to be
searching for entrances until
his solos, when he quietly
turns into brilliant

And Betty, retirement home royalty,
crowned for her
breathing through the decades—

Betty smiles and nods the rhythm
into her next astonishing
beat of
heart

It Was Edna Who Told Me To

Sorrow had transformed her . . .
all my thoughts are slow and brown
and in my world,
the Greek chorus of
white pines outside the window
danced cadenzas of bliss,
in the late autumn's
warm breeze
So I unearthed the washboard
and began my work,
the soaking,
the scrubbing,
the cleansing,
until my thoughts were
almost pure

And I hung them out to dry,
gave them over to the pines
for an afternoon
of line dance lessons

The Bathtub of Coriolanus

International Shakespeare Company
    —Santa Fe 2021 performance

Blood and muscle,
it's a scrubbing of so much,
a lingering as he
recounts, counts
the battles, the wounds,
the Tribunes,
the very nature of Win
as the drive to kill
fades for a moment with
the hot soak,
as the tub holds,
until the draining and
toweling,
the fight tight

Adaptation

You have taken the east from me,
You have taken the west from me
     —Dónal Óg, 8th-century poem

I have become the ice melting
as fast as skating,
I have become the stream freezing
as slow as wild fire

My east held my pierce,
my blaze
The west held my breath,
my fury

With your spinning compass,
look for me now in
the north, fawning,
now in the south,
teeth bared

Smile or threat,
your guess,
not mine anymore

Not mine

Along the Santa Fe Trail

To get to Trader Joe's,
a quick jaunt along
the wagon trail before we
turn onto West Cordova
to grab some baby carrots
and cold brew coffee

Then back into the wagon
with kombucha,
without oxen,
honour and respect
settling in at
each stoplight,
glowing

Accessory to Love

In front of a wall of hats,
most of us wonder,
Are we hat people?

We try on,
like theatre costumes,
assess the transformation,
remember our grandmothers
and usually, return
loveliness back onto the knob,
knowing we can't wear
without a posturing

They were browsing
and stopped,
lured by the soft and round

She tried one on
and turned to her lover
His smile, his beaming
evident from aisles away

He reached for more hats
and tried them on her above
her giggling

They played for a bit,
then floated away,
their joy an accessory
in itself,
dazzling

Free Verse

Auden thinks
more often the result is squalor

On the other hand
I, with no hyphen yet after my birthyear,
believe the Free Verse is
an eleven-year-old city girl,
weekends of inner-city art programs,
museum visits, city park theatre,
and summers on the family farm
with plenty of clean sheets
and crisp apples

Prism

As we caught late afternoon rays
on the banking,
someone's diamond in row seven was
doing a dance on the ceiling
during the descent,
fairies all over and then
gone like a shiver,
like a dreaming,
like a destiny,
brilliant and
flawed

Breakdown

I know my sorrow is such simple chemistry
—Frank X. Gaspar

Living in the beaker as I do,
just above the Bunsen burner,
life can be a series of analyses,
colour variations,
changes of state,
the heat of the moment
always bubbling on
the other lab bench

But when it comes to sadness,
I could draw the reaction
in my sleep, hanging
from monkey bars in
the middle of a hurricane

It's classified so no-one
can use it as a weapon
against me ever again

But, because I have an
itchy mind, I can't help but
sketch a few of the more
attractive molecules in

different poses on
the top of a pin,
remember the pricking

At Three a.m.

      my mind is
  a city dump
            gulls screaming
      bulldozers dozing,
                              bulling

      squalls of thoughts,
                      spinning

I begin the counting of
      genetically-modified sheep as they
      try for their best time in hurdling

      And on the sidelines,
wolves dressed in pinafores

holding stop-watches and knitting needles,
beaming

Name Change

Through the night,
through the howling with
its glissandos of sevenths,
mordents and trills at
the top,
the wind becomes a chorus,
a gather of Gregorian,
chanting about the end of
reign, of cold,
the joy, the power,
with premonition in
the low growls, about
what it takes to
become

        Tornado

The Square Footage of Awe

Did you know
that lichen,
an elegant union of
alga and fungus,
covers six percent of
the earth's non-wat'ry
surfaces?

Six percent, which
makes me wonder
what percentage of
our earth is covered with
jealousy? Indifference?
Rage? Nostalgia?
The rolling hills of Felicity,
A mountain range of Loathing,
and the Admiration prairie,
where we lie down and
breathe without
measurement

First Loss

for Nahla

A joyful one—
the tiniest lower tooth
Tonight, gathered for a birthday,
four generations
witnessed and felt
the wiggly tooth,
then a brave girl
running towards
the mirror

Oz

thanks to Thomas Terry

It doesn't really matter
which has-been star it was,
because it was a great story

The forty-five minutes of a restless,
expectant crowd
The disturbance as four security guards
carried in the drunken ragdoll headliner
and deposited her in the spotlight,
the one that had blinded her
so many times,
the way bravado and self-doubt
can't cancel each other out

The crowd booed.
She tried to sing,
the feeble confused song of
a canary in the coal mine,
slumped over.
Their little angel now a
pickled wash-up

But love,
love restores, doesn't it,
when it's in the right mood
and for this crumpled soul bared,
the audience felt sorrow,
and, sparked by pity,
did what she couldn't.

And as 'Rock-a-Bye' began
to blossom in the theater,
so she did too;
the crawling tattered survivor,
finding the oasis of sustenance, acceptance
and she remembered the voice,
the words, the tunes,
end fluffing her feathers,
staying out of her cage
for three solid beautiful hours,
the magic of ruby red wishing

The Assassin's Son

So shy, quiet,
the perfect second violin in
the Brahms quartet at
music camp in paradise,
bringing out the heartbeat in
a pulsing string of eighth notes

His father,
the wild Russian violin professor,
former KGB assassin
teaching the art of chamber music,
the delicate phrase turn,
crosshairs intonation essential
when playing well with others

Asked by non-assassins
how can he live with himself?
His answer:
a lifetime dedication to
helping children

Teaching and teaching
the sharpshooter details of
a splendid musical life

Eating the Angel's Book

And I took the little book out of the angel's hand and ate it
—Revelation 10:10

I.

In my case,
he told me to eat it raw
and handed over a prescription warning
and a list of possible deadly interactions

In my case,
it seemed to be a chapbook,
so I took it with a bit of sage advice
to fill my belly,
And I'm thinking that's what
turned bitter in my gut

Having never eaten book before
I was ravenous
ripping out the pages and setting some
beneath my tongue,
letting the word's words'
sublingual messages absorb

II.

angel was right
it tasted like whispers
like a meadow
it tasted like birdsong

like midsummer under-the-stars loving
it tasted like peach blossom
like a fanfare of newly-hatched chicks
like a whale's sunrise breaching

I wanted to call in
the restaurant critics,
tell them about dining on book,
the word's succulence
the spice of sentence

but angel put a
feathered finger to his lips,
and the secret
turned
sour

For a Friend in Tasmania

If you have never made a snow angel,
please follow instructions below:

Pick a fresh snowfall,
today, for example,
with snow as light
as a birthday wish,
where Roget can't help you
with the word 'fluffy'

Grab a friend
Find a field, a yard, any
piece of earthsnow
Fall back down,
let the flakes land on
your eyelashes
Then, begin the flight
and the gown construction
and when you are finished,
be an angel for
a few minutes longer,
then ask your friend for a hand
to pull you up,
pull you down from
a five-year-old heaven,
laughing

Viola Lessons

At each lesson,
I'm teaching myself—
the kids play scales,
respond to suggestions,
bow hold, pressure, length,
Drop the left wrist,
swing the elbow towards
its sister, let the fingers
drop down, be there,
ready to march, dance, dazzle

Figure out the geography of
a passage, topography of
the fingerboard, the geometry of
a rhythm: triangle, square,
pentagon

Mostly dos,
but a few don'ts:

Don't be scared of fast,
don't be scared of slow
and don't ever
play without
fire

Yesterday

I could hear
shadows of my
happiness shuffling
behind me,
feel the burn of
hope in my shoulders,
taste a sadness in
a piece of toast
smell the strength of
resolve in your baited breath
and see the birds circle
wildly above me
as I lay within a meadow,
waiting

Today
I sleep
and as I sleep
I shake the earth
with my living,
one harlequin'd breath
at a time

After Reading That Cows Have BFF's

Heart rates,
cortisol levels,
the rhythms of
cud in 4/4

Tale of tails with
swishing of flies

We've got history
And udders
The magic of
bovine bond

So when the scientists are
nowhere to be found,
lean against me,
tell me a milky secret or two
that can't be documented
and let me breathe again
your sweet sweet
clover breath

The Fade

Autumn's reckoning,
as we move towards the core
The wooden naked
watch us reach for others' coats
the sheep's, the llama's

We begin the burrowing
through the soft spirit of
spring and summer towards
the bones of winter,
where brittle songs are sung
and hot dreams are put out on
the porch to cool, their dance now
wildly unstructured as
the wind pushes them to their limit,
a brutal ballet master who used
to be so breezy with praise,
now the tyrant, flipping dreams in
the cold skillet into
a nightmare of sorts

And we feel the bristle of core's
weakening scrape us as we begin
the deliberate wading through
a colder time

Occasional Purpose

I spotted it,
like porpoises
in a bay,
occasionally
but it's always
an occasion—
the flash of eyes
across a counter
gathering you briefly
into a deep unknown,
a blaze of fins
as they stitch
line of ocean,
then lose the
thread,
and you are left,
or leave, with
a shift in
breath,
a tilt in
tableau

Moose Sighting

I had ordered one from
my daughter in Maine;
A whale would be a bonus

I scanned the midnight mists,
the mossy moosey fairy glens
shouldering the bays,
the thawing bogs,
the sleeping forests, all of
which would have been a
perfect glided frame for a moose

Just one,
with or without antlers
but with those astonishing
spindles, remarkable proboscis

But I realized in the search,
there lay the thrill,
so much that I completely
forgot to scan for
sea monsters

Watching

I knew it would
be this way,
the application of
external forces
to the heart's
simplest charge
and as I watched
the snow's soft fall
from up to down,
I fell into my heart
for a few moments
and looked around

A dozen taut ropes or more
tethered to the walls
and I finally understood
the tightness,
the Celtic knotting of
a simple task
and the reverse
centrifugal force of
the heave-ho's
from all those on
my VIP list

Parameters

I'll tell you,
    if you'll listen,
    let me in
    let me out

I'm the dog at the door,
    either side,
        whimper or bark

I'm the snake under the stairs,
    just wanting to be me,
    not your nightmare

I'm the fly,
    buzzing, of course

I'm the toad in your chlorine,
    clueless until it's too late

But mostly,
    I'm the door
    the hinges
    the knob,
    ready for a
    swing

II. Fourteen Acorns and a Vagary

Before the Prologue

Lakeside Shakespeare Theatre,
        —Frankfort, Michigan

Just above the amphitheatre,
deer thread their way
between trees,
busy with languid
deer errands, listening
to warmups, the audience
settling in with
anticipation and picnic
before the stage that holds
tightly to comedy, tragedy

Back and forth, the whitetails
float through the verdant backdrop,
as though they were briefly
stitched into the scenery,
there and gone
just like the young lovers, balconied,
whose unforgettables have
lingered for
centuries

The Art of Dazzle

The earth as I saw it
at daybreak
was a colossal
sugarplum
Even my pet
fruit flies were
drawn to the
window,
flitting about in
a dance of frustration

A light breeze ran
its tongue across
the crystallized
treetops
and I shuddered
with unspeakable
pleasure

Packing for Bucharest

I'm going to Romania
historically blind
so I'll wrap my
ignorance in velvet
and carefully place her
in the egg carton I
always carry in the
suitcase, hoping something will
break on the way home

All I need is a computer for
the presentation,
boots, garlic,
and a mind desperate to capture
the cultural swirls
the darkness of the legends
the legends of darkness
and plenty of imagination
I will conceal from customs
in an uninformed theory,
shimmering

Journey of Flour Butter Sugar

for James Talbot

Because I'm lucky enough to
own a phone,
have a father to bake for,
I could text, call or
check online
their path

I could be a brownie busybody
or even a stalker,
as they cross above
Montana grizzlies,
plains of bison

As they experience turbulence
over the ranges,
then as they land next to
an ocean,
begin their northward progression
towards apartment number
three hundred and thirty-nine,
where a plate and coffee
await their dense
and lovely
homecoming

Blue

When I wane in my swim,
I remember the aquarium pencil's
declaration that the blue whale
is longer than the pool

I become your companion,
blue princess of my childhood,
as I swim along your length and
flip, the last yards back to
the perfection of your tail,
ride the wake of your descent

I dreamswim of stroking
through your massive veins,
a turn through that
behemoth heart,
then I'm back up next to
you and your loveliness,
fluid miles of tireless
companionship ahead

Turning the Late Winter Blues into Red and Yellow

Roast a pepper,
fork held over flame

Slowly turn to
the perfect burn,
satisfaction of rotation,
almost a feeling
of morality,
democracy

Does it feel familiar?
Yes, campfires are just
around the corner of
this blurry, blustery month

This year, there will be
s'mores in April, I promise

without mosquitoes

The Falling

Last night,
thirteen fallen angels
fell into the pool

Most of them were from
the 1500s and barely knew how to swim

But they managed,
tattered wings and all,
hung out in the shallow end

I put out a pitcher of
margaritas and tried to
converse, but only one
spoke broken English,
and my scant old French was
past saving

So I left them to it

In the morning, there were frogs on
the inner tubes, the pitcher was empty,
and a few blue feathers spun around
on the unbroken reflection of
skies above

The Naming

Because I'm so very
fond of them,
I've decided to name
my cups of coffee

This morning's is
French Roast Billy,
or Wilhemina for short
She's so lovely,
with her subtle tones of
smoky sweet and
free-verse mouthfeel

So different from yesterday's
Roger, who only wrote
sonnets, divine and bitter

But most memorable recently is
last week's light roast Angeles,
who won the derby
with a fabulous finish

Last night

without the slightest warning,
a Poem flopped himself
down in my lap
Just assumed I was
an available woman

Maybe it was the
way I twirled
my empty martini glass,
laughing one dynamic
louder than usual,
but the Poem didn't
let me establish
anything further

Simply demanded my
full attention
until I was
finally able to
write him
off

Wild Girl

She flies up onto
the lilac bush
to get a better look at
I don't know,
what does a chicken need to
see from above?

But every day,
with the sound of
a shaken comforter,
her winging announces
sentry duty,
the artist scanning for
material,
the feral dream

If You Go Down Under

Be wary of wallaroos
Listen for the kookaburras' epic histories,
the wild budgies, the dry fathom leaps
of the Big Reds

Looking needs no cues
for there, eyes never want to blink

Inhale the dry gum tree's essence,
the sea's great white perfume—
you'll feel it in your teeth
and when you find a shark's tooth on
the endless glory of beach,
remember the world from whence,
through death, it emerged,
where I used to swim until the lifeguard's
third call to clear the water *because of*

And if you get to the edge of the Outback,
blow it a quiet kiss from me,
and a song and a howl

But most importantly,
show my sent heart a flash of childhood,
beach and all,

then rewrap it in brown paper and vinegar,
put it back in its inscrutable case
and send it back
on a slow slow boat

Fourteen Acorns and a Vagary

Maybe it was fifteen
falling and bouncing
from the park bench—
too many squirrels
distracting the count,
a requiem in oak minor
for a century of service,
sciurus as ushers,
no choir,
just the pizzicato
of release,
libretti of
rustle and
drop

Garden Experiment Number Seventy-Two

One year, I tried planting
a row of confidence
in the stunning earthy wealth
from the last year's kitchen

Dreamed of a sauté,
with garlic and a dash of
organically-neglected *je ne sais quoi,*
a hearty side dish for the
psyches of daughters three

But one night, when the
silence of the owl was deafening,
and the star songs
unbearably beautiful,
the nefarious garden warriors
stormed the chicken wire citadel
and feasted

So all I had to show for that season
was a stunning crop of tomatoes,
platoons of squash blossoms,
vampire radishes, and a garden full of
dauntless rodents

At the Aquarium

Wear polka dots and stripes
to make the viewed regard you
with comradery

Forget there is glass

Become the shark,
then glide through
peaceable kingdoms,
not eating your friends
in front of the pressed children

Slide into the snake's skin
coil, then slither into
eighty percent of nightmares

Be a dolphin, rocketing
up to the surface world,
leap

Giant cockroach,
the stench
and repel

Waddle a bit with
the waddlers then
finish the visit with
a transformation—

Become the unnoticed
minnow, hide and
flourish

Hemming Caesar's Trousers

We all know she's going to
die in the first scene of act three,
but she can't die tripping on
her Savers' trousers, so
I snip, press, and stitch

And as I hem with the stitch
my grandmother's hands taught me,
life tightens up a bit
with each slipping
of needle

Forward, with reverse stitches
to hold, like a dance step,
like a step towards
the building of
an empire

Today You Are a Museum Wing

Gilded frames hang around each eye,
catching the glare of your gaze

Today, your nonsensical nose
sports a 17th-century dark Spanish frame
You smell, smell like,
saffron, garlic,
good intentions

Your cheekbones have
a wall unto themselves,
hung high and inaccessible

For this exhibit,
smiles have been put in
storage, wrapped and cloistered

And your mouth today has
no frame in its gallery of
humming and chanting,
lips parted with suggestions of
snarl, good will, and
edged benevolence

Finding

I find myself a table and chair
—Leonard Cohen

In the café
I find I have become

I melt into the origin
hot chocolate,

my quads become
the table's shapely legs

I face the becoming menu
and become its basic superlative,

coarse as courses,
the way of the trumpet,
a palette of proclaim

Vaccination with Anna

Nobody came to meet me with a lantern
  —Anna Akhmatova

I had my flickering moral flashlight on
for days, seeking an appointment and
I found one at last—
a time slot in a nearby town

I needed a warrior with me—
what good is one warrior alone?
Plus, I had the post-shot wait so
I grabbed a volume of Akhmatova
> *On to my right hand I fumbled the*
> *glove to my left hand*
After the moats and dragons at
the pharmacy window,
the castle door opened and
the white-coated pharmacist
called my name
> *And she was like a white flag*
> *. . . in the light of a beacon*

After the shot, I waited with Anna—
I found a poem she wrote
the month I got my first name

And then I walked to my car with
that hamsterwheel feeling of
triumph and disbelief

> *so many stones are*
> *thrown at me,*
> *they no longer scare*

And I sang all the way home

*Akhmatova's quotes are in italics

Storm While Hiking

As scary as going up the
basement stairs as a child,
was the running down the
mountain this time,
watching the storm descend like
a plane's arrival 15,000 feet,
14,000 feet, 13,000 feet

We all knew the mother in town
with the lightning scar along
her side, the mother who had
lost her only son on the mountain
just across the local map
from where we were

We had followed the formula,
the regional adage of up the mountain early,
but the thunderheads appeared
like unexpected warriors
and chased us with their roaring,
biting our heels with lightning
down past the tree line

Self-preservation was put aside
to help the more deliberate friends
behind me, carrying their packs,
trying to comfort, encourage,
whatever could change the tempo
of their descent so I wouldn't be the one
left with the scar and
festering guilt of
survivor

Self-Portrait

Today's is sketched
with a tongue-licked
finger pressed into
the red dust of
the Outback

The wet and dry of
my childhood—
in the ocean,
the arid *Bush*
with a cast of sharks, kangaroos,
sting after sting of jellyfish,
bite after bite of spider,
a survival, thriving in
a paradise of peril

Still, two good enough eyes,
very few scars,
only a couple of shattered hearts,
and not a single
broken
bone

Behemoth

The captain tells us of
the biggest,
the wave he remembered
almost like the deepest love,
so high and fast and fierce,
hanging on for the dearest
life of all, yours,
as you cling with colleagues,
the ocean versus
a handful of biceps at the helm,
and you win in a way that
you know isn't a victory,
just a moment of,
a murmur of
planetary grace,
given

Lined

Shoulder to shoulder
in apron shimmy,
our pegged stripes can melt a bit
in the breezes unexpected

A line dance, a chorus line,
along the radish row

Clouds and sparrows shooed
as we become an indolent part
of evaporation's crisper gavotte,
our light steps an upbeat to Dry

Alive

House full of hot vinegar,
coffee pots cleaned,
cat bowls scrubbed
The brilliance of
vyn egre—
old French, sour wine—
in my eyes, my breaths
Alive!
And with this feeling,
gratitude for
the tweakers of fermentation,
the ancient Babylonians
with their dates, figs
and primordial
patience

III. Plainsong

Translation

There is no better definition of
Wait than this morning's sky

Even the crows are staying in the trees,
pausing their retching and sketching

It could be snow today—
that heavy hanging stillness

This midwinter sky today
a blank gray page,

Open and ready for
the next story

Rumours of Dementia

His last concert
maybe,
as he frantically asks
his backstage support team
What am I playing?
The thirteenth?

Oh god, it looks like cyrillic!
But manages to focus and
perform a gnarly fugue

Those of us who know,
imagine the brain battles,
watch him win

And afterwards,
chatting,
he remembers
and remembers
and remembers,
the memories like
prisms, turning
and turning in
the sun,
dazzling

Caught

It's a question of faith
—the days when you can
think only of love or
calculus, you leave the rest to
the organist who dutifully
improvises a prefatory in the spirit
of some great German,
an involuntary in B,
towards the blinking, the pulsing,
a breathy tango of oxygen
and its toxic partner,
drawn together then released
A chorale of muscle,
the voiced blending
for the cloistered ambulatory
so you can fall
where the softness
of distraction can
catch you,
just
in
time

My Daughter Laughed

for Izzie

and said she
could only hear
her boots
but couldn't you hear
it too?

The prairie swelling,
the dark and trembling crescendo in
the thawing earth
as the bilateral state
begins to unfurl
towards
away
and I begin
to remember
the shock value
of
green

Clothespin Nightlife

They hang like
ripe fruit,
waiting for a
twist, a
release, listening to
the owl song,
then back to
the morning's joyful grip,
dancing, conserving
under the scallop of
goldfinch

A Brief Brief History of a Snowball

We could talk about
sintering,
mean kids,
Faraday,
his ice particle studies
of attraction

But how about we
stand at the top of
a snowy slope with
snowflake mittens knitted
by great-aunt Jean
and begin the scoop and
pat and roll about a bit,
then the launch
down the hill and
watch the gathering,
so much like,
if you are as lucky as
a snowball,
the ontogeny of
love

The Gathering

for Bruce

A child is lost

The trumpets scream their wailing fanfare
and the world is awake

It knows what it needs to do
and how little time there is,
because at these moments
there is no time

No time to remember to breathe,
so it sends its oxygen to those who have lost theirs

No time to remember happiness,
so it calls forth the sheepdogs
and love is effortlessly herded together,
with not even a bark, nor a nip,
and marches onto a low-lying cloud
and floats towards the loss,
gathering the cherishing

And after a tender ethereal aria,
the world lets love's bold infirmity and sorrow's strength
fall through its open hands

gently down upon the grieving
and charred pieces of grief
are silently gathered by friends,
carried for those who have lost,
for those whose burden is
unspeakable

Plainsong

I

Gray
the clouds began
to proceed
across the sky
darkening the world for an afternoon
in pairs of three
pewter trios of two
and a huge, agitated crowd
of one

II

Gray
the sidewalks
crack around their history
mothers' backs
brutal winters
blistering summers
the dog prints
and the leaf that dropped
half a season early,
cemented into the embrace
of drying perimeters

III

Gray
the feather
now plumage
for the fence's barb.
No more rules
of engagement,
the corps dancer's
duty to catch a draft
in the troupe of structure
no more the
prevailing westerly
oarsmen flying solo now
to the wind's song

Raven

So black the feather,
its colour is not
even mentioned in
the Field guide's
respectful narrative

Even with the words
flapping
  shaggy
 goiter
       croaking
       bones,

studs in the story,
we know that
there is nothing common
about the
Common Raven

The Bone's Story

It was hardly an
epic tale,
just a simple story
of a life, a death
and the enviable
in-between

I held the bone
against my cheek,
let the heat
of its world
burn into my pores,
held it up
to my ear,
let the white song
fall into *my* manuscript
and with a sigh,
I kept the story going

Burying the Cat

We knew exactly where
to begin the digging
beneath the beneath of window,
the blade framing the bed
and as we built,
we remembered,
and as we remembered
we understood . . .

the way the ancient Egyptians
enclosed a journey in
their chambered farewells
and we sprinkled
the sweet wrap of cat
with food, words, flowers,
a companion's fur,
the old can of tuna, and
bowers of fresh catnip

And with each blade full,
we buried the waiting,
packed down the pity,
let the rain's whisper
sprinkle the buried
with a farewell's
veiled momentum

A Close Read

Though I felt like
simply flipping the pages,
I tried to read
the earth this
morning,
the careless snow setting
down its
nine-dimensional fable
through the woods
Sideways a fast story
in Hebrew,
180° tilt and it's an
endless Latin conjugation

But, have you ever
watched the snowfall
upside down?
Maybe it's the blood rushing to
the head, but tell me
if you heard what I did,
a spotless Hallelujah chorus
of full-tongued silence?

Two Pairs

Walked down to the river,
under Harbor Drive,
along Water Ave. and
SW Moody

But this isn't about geese,
their tiny beaches,
their swift downstream races

It's about the two pairs of pants
dancing on the sidewalk as
I passed one of the tent towns

Gavotte, gigue,
then shimmy as they lay
in the midday heat,
in the reverie of dream,
happy, today,
to be
forgotten

In the High Desert Pool

walled by Southwest stucco,
the view is water, wall, sky

and that trio above:
A raven careening towards
the wafer of a morning moon,
across a brilliant
breathtaking blue

And I fall back into
the wetter blue and float,
dissolving the sky with
each brushy stroke

Eldorado Nights

The mourning doves have
ceased their lamentation,
the cholla's piercing silhouette
has faded behind an indigo curtain

What is left of a busy
day has settled onto
a branch deep in the juniper

Now the moon
begins to oversee this
high desert of eyeshine and coil,
rustle and howl

And over the hill,
a fanfare of yip as
the triumph of a kill
crescendos into the paving
of our dreams,
bumpy paths of
fang and footfall

Out Here

every night a clear night,
a bath of stars

Milky Way leading
up to your front door

Saturn til 3:27 a.m.
and all night long,
Neptune slow dancing

Below,
no white picket
delineation, just
space, spaces
between,
around,
as you fall up into
a delicious uncertain,
trembling

Unseasonably

They seemed more appropriate
for a spring holiday,
but there they were
every Christmas, deep
in their cookie-jar coop—
anise seed chick cookies
with a sunny brushed-yolk coat,
then out,
peeping through cold
afternoons, often next to
a glass of milk,
gone too soon

Clean Death

for Eve Robillard

She emerged from the bird bath
and flew right into the heaven
that is reserved for birds that
fly into the blazing world of
a window's embrace

Every morning
her ghost reappears,
clean and dripping on
the kitchen window

So every morning
Miss Eve has coffee with
an angel

Flamed

I watch last night's
birthday candles
float in the custard dish,
a dozen white candles
bobbing like bartered brides

The wax has melted through
fanfare, wish, blow,
just enough left for
another celebration

And washed,
they settle back into
the designated jar,
resting bright eyes,
idling until
the next cue

I Remember

before I could breathe again,
before I could see a path ahead,
the weight of five little letters,
g,r,i,e, and f

And now,
when I think of you,
you're a zephyr,
passing,
a name in my candle,
flaring,
a minor third in the chord,
blooming

How Time with her bandages
and balms manages
so well to palliate,
open eyes,
apply oxygen,
pull us up into a position of
walking forward,
sometimes remembering
how to skip

Diversion

Today, for example,
the blast of Saint-Saens'
organ symphony we play next week

So loud in my head,
some days, the music,
that I forget which drawer
the socks are dozing in,
in which cupboard
the clean plates are welcome

Then the blast of
a phrase finishes, fades
as my brain comes up
for air
and I can return to
folding the plates,
stacking the socks,
remember where
the floor is, and
how to walk
again

Red Onion Politic

The way it can
gracefully add
its biting opinions to
the lettuce,
reveal policy in
a slaw

And its suggestion of a
rambler rose strategy
across a plate of
sliced citrus,
singing loudly,
but always in tune

Bass at Rest

The harpsichord has
taken over—
it's Brandenburg five,
after all,
where she slowly crawls in
like a fog and
soon is the only one singing—
and the bass player stands
like a Roman statue,
his hand draped over
the instrument
like a lover,
waiting for the cadence
along with the rest of
the statues until
the spell is broken
and Bach puts himself back
together

Trill

It's a quavering,
the fingers flying
between semitones

Technically,
a lift and landing
so practice on a pencil,
practice on a fork,
don't take a day off

Hard work to
sound easy,
the ripple,
the suspension,
a fingered bridge to
the next story

Along the Interstate,

a few rundown,
long-in-the-tooth
trailers in an
ancient trailer park

And one graced with a
grand gazebo,
a snatch of kingdom to
place where you
can

In the Hills Above Santa Fe

The chilies hang from
the porch

The breeze brings in
piñon

And I sit,
breathing with
lizard and
buzz of plane,
liquid sextuplets of
spotted towhee,
thinking about
breathing,
listening

These are
the gifts
of this
land

Minus Six and I Make Tea

Green, with a single leaf of
dried mint from last summer

And I'm back,
floating on the northern lake
where I dug up some
shoreline mint years ago,
the sun baking my prone
air mattress body

I spin gently in the heat,
a vortex of dozy pleasure,
my fingers singing adagios
through warm waters,
imagining the colder
world months away,
the comfort of tea,
the necessary mint to
spark the cycle

Aspirational Fashion

the dress hanging from her shoulders like bad geometry
—Dorianne Laux

I want a ballgown
as big as the ballroom.
Alice's tonic, filling up
the glittering hall,
pushing out the elegance of
couples, knocking out
the orchestra with a graceful turn,
the tinkle of
champagne flutes shattering,
as I feel the power of
dancing alone

Tonight

Yonder has
chosen a stunning pewter
satin to drag along behind her,
an alluring train of shimmer
as she walks ahead of you,
in what looks to be about
a quarter of a mile

Why, I ask, aren't you
running?

About the Author

Australian-born Katrin Talbot's collection *The Devil Orders a Latte* was just released from Fernwood Press. *Falling Asleep at the Circus* (Turning Point Books, 2024) and *The Waiting Room for the Imperfect Alibis* (Kelsay Books, 2022) are her other full-length collections. She has seven chapbooks, two Pushcart Prize nominations, and quite a few chickens. Ms. Talbot is also a violist and photographer, and her coffee table book, *Schubert's Winterreise-A Winter Journey in Poetry, Image, and Song,* was published by the University of Wisconsin Press in 2003. She plays in the viola section of the Madison Symphony Orchestra and often the Wisconsin Chamber Orchestra, and there is much music in her poetry as a result of this.

Website: katrintalbot.com
Instagram: @ktalbot21

www.ingramcontent.com/pod-product-compliance
Lightning Source LLC
Chambersburg PA
CBHW030051170426
43197CB00010B/1481